The Night with James Dean

The Night with James Dean and Other Prose Poems
© Allison A. deFreese / Cathexis Northwest Press

No part of this book may be reproduced without written permission of the publisher or author, except in reviews and articles.

First Printing: 2022

Paperback ISBN: 978-1-952869-71-6

Cover design by C. M. Tollefson
Cover art © Allison A. deFreese, "Trilogy V," 2018
Editing by C. M. Tollefson & Airea Johnson

Cathexis Northwest Press

cathexisnorthwestpress.com

The Night with James Dean
and Other Prose Poems
by Allison A. deFreese

Cathexis Northwest Press

To Frida

I am grateful to the following publications in which versions of individual works in this chapbook, first appeared, including:

The Bangalore Review,
"Heritage Days"

Exposition Review,
"Star Party" (runner up, ER's 2022 "Escape" theme contest)

Margin: Exploring Contemporary Magical Realism,
"The Heart Postcard"

NUNUM - A Canadian Literary Journal Dedicated to Flash Fiction,
"Proper"

Permafrost,
"Bacon" and "Contributor's Note"

Penn Review,
"Catfish"

Poems and Plays,
"Bouquet"

Quick Fiction,
"Janitor's Kitchen"

Rattle
(online social media page, by invitation of the editors),
"New Moon"

Southeastern Review,
winner of The World's Best Short-Short Story Competition,
"The Night with James Dean"

Many thanks also to friends and colleagues who read earlier versions of selected pieces from this book (in some cases decades ago), including Jill Alexander, Chad Bartlett, Elizabeth Beechwood, Thomas Fuller, Becca Hardwick, Faith Helma, Terry Lopez, Jacquolyn McMurray, Naomi Shihab Nye, Christina Pfister, Katherine Quevedo . . . and especially . . . Lora K. Reiter and David A. Wevill.

Table of Contents

Catfish	23
Bacon	24
The Night with James Dean	26
Star Party	27
Proper	28
Heritage Days, 2020	29
Janitor's Kitchen	30
I Can't Find My Life Vest	31
The Prose Poem	32
The Heart Postcard	33
Bouquet	34
Buqué	35
Mask	36
One Night by the River	37
New Moon	38
Contributor's Note	40

Catfish

In one life I came back as the cake at a catfish wedding. It was deep August in the muddy bottom where the Missouri nibbled a piece of Kansas at the Kaw.

Blues and channel cats longer than bridal trains swam both sides of the current. The flower girls were bullheads with freckles, their bouquets snags strung with veils.

The pastor was a six-foot flathead. He wore hooks in his whiskers, as if piercings, and had been around long enough to snap a few lines. He ate the little ring bearer at once, along with the rings. They were, after all, both only ceremonial and guests kept leaving to spawn in a tributary.

The buffet smelled like rancid liver. And I was prettier than I had ever been. I was trussed up and proper, a petticoat in three layers, my soul external like a crayfish shell. A painted lady trimmed in buttercream; my icing once white began rising in bubbles before anyone opened the bubbly. My flour from so many wheat sprigs came unraveled next. I was a mass again, indistinguishable from raindrops in the river, from a tear landing on the sandbank or a sneeze that can never be called back midair, a few last words, a life vest, a pledge.

By the time they said their vows, I'd dissolved into a waxy film. Slowly I drifted upward before settling in the flotsam, then silently sailed on toward another sunset.

Bacon

You can bring back a frozen piglet from the dead. Find even the hint of a tick in her stiff side, and you may manage to revive her. The litter born in the open, fastened on the ground, on the rare January morning when you are off school on a raw day after a blizzard, your road a tunnel of gravel through banks of snow, or the road ungraded and rising white between the windrows.

You discover this brood in the last pen at the edge of the lane, frozen in the shapes of miniature pigs as if Christmas cookies stuck to the tray or a flat nativity. The baby hair, that would have later bristled, sticks up like little waves on a cold ocean. The placenta, delivered late, still steams like a new island.

The sow lies on her side under the shelter, clucking her mother song. How did you all miss the signs last night? Why didn't you bring this hog inside in time to farrow in a stall, under a lamp, bedded in a nest of straw feathers?

You unstick the tiniest from her birth ice and lift her, cat-sized and pink, press your hand against the quick of the belly bacon to feel for the slightest quack, for the click of heartbeat behind that delicate cage fine as fish ribs, then carry the rigid newborns in a blanket back to the kitchen. You fill a red bucket with warm water as hot as you can stand it, hotter than a baby's bottle, and submerge your arm with the piglet slowly, up to the elbow until only her eraser nose pokes out above the water, surprisingly soft on the first day and more a fabric sample than a snout for sorting corn cobs in muddy pebbles under the crib.

And you wait for the flicker of lashes, for the oddly human eyelids to twitch or travel behind the dream reels. For the suckling sounds as the mouth unthaws and comes alive to accept at last your pinky—though you withdraw your finger, tender as a nipple, when you feel the needle teeth—as would any mammal, warm and in search of milk and mammary. And bringing her back from the frozen afterlife in these fifteen minutes while holding her brother with your left hand in another bucket, you lay her by the radiator in an apple box filled with hay. You guide her toward the bottle filled with colostrum collected at a previous farrowing; she accepts it as if from memory. And watching without the slightest thought of eating her, you see this small creature, alive again, feeding fragile and breathing, before you reach for another heart to thaw.

The Night with James Dean

She tells anyone who'll listen. The story, genderless and sexy as a dollhouse teddy bear, never changes. She wanted to be an actress. One night, an extra on the set, she went home with Jimmy. They made it at his place. He was *a shy boy, so bashful*, and *not as tall as you'd think*. A year, later she posed for *Playboy*. That was it; she never acted or modeled again.

Her story ends sixty-six years ago, and she's never broken character. Sighing, she looks up into the dark, dark hours, scanning the sky for distant stars and silver spiders.

Star Party

Vivien streams her dress of cascade and applegreen. She turns into a shooting star tonight. There are candles in the sky. She sails toward them in a violin case that opens like a scallop shell and once held music and treasure. Her spoon overflows with ants and twinkling fish teeth. Her oar, a plastic shovel, spills a line of sand old as the world. There are diamonds in it, a trail back to somewhere unremembered but not forgotten. For a moment she sees the whole universe, before blinking. She holds suns by the billions in each iris. Vivien wears her dress of water and leaves, the color of planets when she spins. Vivien turns into a shooting star tonight—not five—her hair already a starpart curling upward in flames rolling on ocean, bowing and lifting like horses as they stomp and whinny in the wind. Her lips melt in a starsparkle so fizzy it doesn't hurt her; her mouth a beam of lipstick smeared in starlight from the tail of her paintbrush, dripping at the troth. Vivien turns into a star tonight and you have never seen a shooting start like this one. You have never seen a shooting star like this one. She is going off in a shower of sparklers because a star is actually a tree and honey tastes like flowers, not bees. Vivien plants a seed in the galaxy and blows out wishes. And she knows. She will not grow up to be just any field or forest.

Proper

It was a proper funeral. Live pipers played requiems to her ash and the sermon brimmed with fireplace trifles, tea cozies, scones with real cream. Omitted: the middle husbands; the stepdaughter, disinherited, who'd also passed that summer, alone, living with cats in a van; and the deeper secrets old friends kept buried.

Her last weeks, she'd crashed the Mercedes into the garage wardrobe and left a card at the temple to seal Rufus. She thought him too long gone to notice, but Rufus knew. He was a hummingbird now, wild and red; his soul had already escaped into the fuchsias.

Heritage Days, 2020

An inheritance means someone is missing, and you are next—poorer in years than in photos or paper if this was your progenitor. You sit stunned on the family loveseat too large for your apartment, calculating your span and the gap stretching long beneath the flapping chasm of a generation. Heredity, then, the riches of blooming or booming when odds were you would never be planted, a final sneeze and the night of your conception dissolves in air, an aspirin in water. You might not have held full term like the twin sisters before you, floating off with their cords like small pink balloons; and your grandmother in labor three days with your father in 1939, poisoning each other's blood for hours, neither might have arrived at the crowning. And what if her mother, your great-grandmother—bringing with her only a kitchen chair caned in the old world, had gone down on the boat from Prussia in 1917—or if, having spanned the Atlantic, Ellis Island had been shuttered, the border closed. Or if her arrival had been delayed a year and she had caught an avian strain—like your great-grandfather in Nebraska, on the pious side, would in 1918— his lungs filling like a mossy well one autumn a month before the war's end, losing consciousness on the last day, wandering in and out of heaven and deserts while they dabbed his fever dry, his stiff collar loosened, cornered in pneumonia's chokehold. He was thirty-five. The set unmendable. Though their genes—and yours—somehow survived centuries of husbandry and husband stitches and labor, your grandfather, a March baby, and his winter brothers could never have been sown in 1919.

Janitor's Kitchen

The baker sailed off without me in the night. He'd saved our dry bread crusts for weeks, it turns out, and fastened them all together to make a little boat—just big enough for one. I found him pushing off the shore, using a long flat noodle as his oar. Well, go then, I said, Go. And take all the bread you like! Just leave me enough for my morning toast. Call me old-fashioned, but I like it dry. The crust cuts my inner-cheek sometimes, but I don't mind the taste of me so much. Even cheese has the sad flavor of heartmusk here.

He left me the heel of an old French loaf and I scraped it clean of soft white crumbs until it was a hollow bowl. I sat down in it and rocked for long, long time. I didn't notice as the sun set and the tide rose and next thing I knew, I was bobbing on the ocean, the deck of my crusty boat unraveling into sponge. I whipped off my apron and raised it as a sail.

My plan is to sail east northeast and beat him to the coast. I'll conk the lass he's left me for with a kaiser and throw her scarf around my hair. I'll be the one waiting there, swinging a basket of strawberries, a carnation stuck somewhere, my legs shaved to lemon shine. He'll be too short for me, of course, but I'll slouch with shyness. And if our union doesn't work out, there's always the next life.

That time we were dogs, that was worst of all, but even as mollusks we just didn't make it.

I Can't Find My Life Vest

Her hair lulls along, just under the water, a deep dull red. She is surfacing again. I am swimming, swimming, frenzied American, eyes the cheap blue of aquarium pebbles. There are her hands. They are fish tails. Jealousy floats about me like ambergris.

She is sure to wash up on some warm beach, off Jamaica, along the Florida Keys he will find her, lift the ark of her hip bones, people her with his half teaspoon universe. Meanwhile, my heart washes up off the coast of Alaska, strangled by sixpack plastic, shuddering in oil, webbed feet still kicking

. . .

The Prose Poem

      The prose poem wears a red bra. One can just make out the straps through a translucent fabric, not quite transparent. It is raining. A pineapple reclines on the table next to two dragon fruits. Out the window, an archetype walks arm in arm with a metaphor, exhaling smoke similes from their cigarettes. The street, poorly lit, leads to a stone fountain full of pennies or a preposition at the end of a sentence as the lamp on the corner flickers out. Soon a second article of clothing will appear or disappear and another color, a cup of wine or glass of coffee. Then a line of dialogue, followed by a question: How does it end?

      Taking silence as a reply, the prose poem begins anew. Fresh laundry smells linger with ships in the fog while the prose poem slides out of his turquoise blue slip.

The Heart Postcard

Oh, oh, oh! Her chest was pounding so hard, she was sure it would explode. The ribs were on the verge of splitting like a brandy barrel. That little puckered radish, her heart, usually not much bigger than a Valentine's candy, had sprouted overnight and grown and grown. It was now closer in size to a pumpkin than an artichoke. She had never been this full of herself. A madness took root in her heart and vines crawled out of her mouth and ears as forget-me-nots shot from her eyes. She'd forgotten how open a face is, really, so many pits and pores. And none could release this pressure pushing out her chest. So she took a thin kitchen knife from the drawer and slowly pressed the tip, just the tip of it, between her third and fourth ribs. No pain from the cut, there was no blood, but a bright orange light streamed from the slit with the slow hiss of air as she collapsed.

Here come the mice who will hide in my husk.
Birds were already carrying off the seeds.

Bouquet

I've inhaled these peonies petal by petal, sniffed until there's nothing left. They are empty now, smell of paper or tap water.

I lost my smile and my soul sneaked out, creeping down my lips, swinging her small pink suitcase.

Buqué

He inhalado estas peonías pétalo por pétalo, las aspiré sin dejar residuo alguno. Ahora están vacías, con olor a papel o a agua.

Perdí mi sonrisa y mi alma se escapó, a hurtadillas, arrastrándose furtiva por mis labios, balanceando su maletita rosa.

translated by Alcira García-Vassaux

Mask

Behind the mask an orange fish swims coyly into your mouth.

This happens quietly, behind the curtain, and no one knows besides the carp and you. How like you not to speak up this time either. You tell yourself it doesn't matter; you were already silent. You have been for a very long time. Your silence echoes, cavernous, its vibrations reach Mars.

How comforting, then, to feel your heart fill to the tip of your little finger, to hear its beat in your ear on the pillow. In the depths of the seashell, an exhale.

One Night by the River

One of them stepped on my foot.

And I said, "Ouch," and then, "I'm sorry! I am so, so sorry."

I'm from rural Kansas, a polite tribe. Tolerance is my faith and besides, my foot was in the way.

My toe only swelled a little from the stomp, but then, it was summer. I was swollen anyway. Drops of water rose on my arms that humid evening as teenage cicada buckled their ribs, crickets scraped legs, and the whippoorwill spoke of *winter's will*, said *it's winter's will*.

Later, as they tied me to the stake and the world went up in flame, I forgave them. I was smiling and being nice. I turned the other cheek, the other half of the hamburger bun. I was apple red but not embarrassed. An apple, a tomato. Nightshade.

Then they ran out of kindling. They had fallen all the trees and kept flicking their lighters like fireflies. Since my shoes had melted together, I became a mermaid. No one noticed as I floated away with driftwood in freshwater. I was already invisible.

New Moon

To María *Luisa Helen Frey* Pereyra

This life I'm in the garden with Louisa Helen eating honey and candied oranges. It's before her wedding and death, but suddenly we must flee when bees start swarming the sugar on our mouths; they think we're candles and want us back in the comb, maybe.

I surface in the slick universe again and alone. It's the morning after New Year's Eve. Everything is sickened or saddened. Rose stems or roman rockets drop like cigar ends, while birds flash silver against a stormy sky and time escapes in the large stack of halved oranges, their pulp pale now as the feeble breeze. Who wouldn't take a scissors to this setting moon, could it be pared or ribboned? If the rind might unwind to yield a bit of predawn cheese?

And I watch the city silhouette in a first low green, turn blue with dabs of fresh peach at the horizon, a tongue-colored shell thrown up from the sea, the streets blanched and beached now for a very long time.

I head back in my flats and my planet-colored dress, a long walk falling somewhere between ankles and knees, swooping in one piece, hems of music. I hear the swish, the ocean, thirty-five degrees C with mixed beauty forecast on the first day.

What a drought in the teacup, this breakfast. Whose lipstick on the hardboiled eggshell? As if I have suffered. I didn't want to sleep in that bed anyway, in a room where strangers' dreams are mixed up in the pillows. The bees back at daybreak still think me sweet; docile in the airy flowers, mellow and sunny under the table, drinking nectar from the pits behind my knee-caps because the earth is new and round today: a sailor's cap without the anchor, the toecap on a freshly polished shoe.

Contributor's Note

Allison A. deFreese grew up on a pig farm. She raised ducks and chickens and had over thirty cats. She learned to impersonate birds and kittens, which brought mother cats running from their secret summer nests so she could find their kitties. Though not an anti-vaxxer (her grandmother deaf in one ear from measles), she has two scars from childhood vaccinations gone bad, a mark on her thumb from building a rabbit cage, and was knocked unconscious by a fall from a horse at age nine (no one knew Lucky had been a rodeo racer and roper). She placed in a state writing contest before dropping out of the sixth grade. She has no high school credits to her name but has taught in high schools—where students in such places are still planning their escape.

Based in the Pacific Northwest, Allison deFreese coordinates multi-language literary translation workshops for the Oregon Society of Translators and Interpreters. Her work appears in *Fireweed: Poetry of Oregon*, *Hunger Mountain*, *La Piccioletta Barca*, *Plainsongs*, and *Waxwing*. Her chapbook *Nurdles and Other Poems* is forthcoming late 2022.

Also Available from Cathexis Northwest Press:

Something To Cry About
by Robert Krantz

Suburban Hermeneutics
by Ian Cappelli

God's Love Is Very Busy
by David Seung

that one time we were almost people
by Christian Czaniecki

Fever Dream/Take Heart
by Valyntina Grenier

The Book of Night & Waking
by Clif Mason

Dead Birds of New Zealand
by Christian Czaniecki

The Weathering of Igneous Rockforms in High-Altitude Riparian Environments
by John Belk

If A Fish
by George Burns

How to Draw a Blank
by Collin Van Son

En Route
by Jesse Wolfe

sky bright psalms
by Temple Cone

Moonbird
by Henry G. Stanton

southern athiest. oh, honey
by d. e. fulford

Bruises, Birthmarks & Other Calamities
by Nadine Klassen

Wanted: Comedy, Addicts
by AR Dugan

They Curve Like Snakes
by David Alexander McFarland

the catalog of daily fears
by Beth Dufford

Shops Close Too Early
by Josh Feit

<u>Vanity Unfair and Other Poems</u>
by Robert Eugene Rubino

<u>Destructive Heresies</u>
by Miloh E. Gorgevska

<u>Bodies of Separation</u>
by Chim Sher Ting

<u>About Time</u>
by Julie Benesh

Cathexis Northwest Press

www.ingramcontent.com/pod-product-compliance
Lightning Source LLC
Chambersburg PA
CBHW050335120526
44592CB00014B/2199